W9-AUG-432

50 fabulous CHAIRS

*I*f you love the unique style of hand-painted chairs, but thought you would have to pay expensive boutique prices ... sit back, relax, and let us show you how to create your own decorator accents at a fraction of the cost!

Anyone can transform orphaned chairs, worn-out family hand-me-downs, flea-market finds, and unfinished furniture into designer showpieces! With just a little paint or a new fabric seat cover, battered or drab-looking chairs can easily be turned into one-of-a-kind treasures that reflect your personality.

Complete crafting how-to's and step-by-step instructions guide you through the restoration process. In addition to the beautiful up-close photography, we've also included full-color patterns for ease in painting. Even beginner-level crafters can customize their own charming chairs.

Express your individuality with Bright Expectations or one of the 49 other designs in a variety of styles, including classic, country, contemporary, and whimsical. With the many fantastic chair ideas in this book, you'll definitely want to "pull up a seat!"

seating

arrangement

delicate touches

You will need a wooden ladder-back chair; ivory, taupe, and pink acrylic paints; floral motif fabric to decoupage and make cushion; cushion form to fit chair seat; 1¹/₂ yds of 1"w ivory satin ribbon; spray adhesive; paintbrushes; primer; sealer; and any additional supplies listed in Step 1.

1. Read Preparing to Paint, Painting Your Chair, and Painting Details, page 54.

2. Prepare chair for painting. Paint chair using ivory paint. Paint top of chair back spindles using taupe and pink paints.

3. Paint edges of chair back rungs using pink paint. Add taupe dots to legs and chair back. Paint taupe stripes on chair back rungs.

4. Cut motifs from fabric; use spray adhesive to attach motifs to chair back rungs. Shade around motifs using taupe paint.

5. Apply sealer to chair.

6. Place cushion form on wrong side of fabric; mark placement of chair back ties on fabric. Cut out two pieces of fabric 2" larger on all sides than cushion. Cut ribbon into

Continued on pg. 57

You will need a wooden arm chair; pink, black, white, light green, medium green, coral, grey, purple, brownish yellow, and yellow acrylic paints; glazing medium; black, medium-point marker; paintbrushes; primer; sealer; and any additional supplies listed in Step 1.

1. Read Preparing to Paint, Painting Your Chair, Transferring Patterns, and Painting Details, page 54.

2. Prepare chair for painting. Paint chair back and seat yellow. Paint seat rim and center chair back spindles light green. Paint armrests coral. Paint chair back spindles, arm supports, legs, and leg braces grey, coral, light green, and yellow. Paint dots and dot flowers on legs, seat, arm supports, and chair back spindles using purple, white, pink, yellow, and coral paints.

3. Apply sealer to chair.

4. Mix four parts glaze to one part brownish yellow paint. Paint chair.

5. Transfer patterns, page 61, to chair back, seat, armrests, center leg brace,

Continued on pg. 57

quilt-patch rocker

You will need a wooden shield-back rocking chair with removable cushion; white, red, and blue acrylic paints; fabric for seat, chair back cushion, and quilt-block appliqué (see table, page 57); buttons; welting; batting; paper-backed fusible web; poster board; newspaper; hot glue gun; paintbrushes; primer; sealer; and any additional supplies listed in Step 1.

1. Read Preparing to Paint, Painting Your Chair, and Covering a Seat, page 54.

2. Prepare chair for painting. Paint chair white. Add details using red and blue paint.

3. Apply sealer to chair.

4. Cover seat.

5. For chair back cushion, draw around chair back on newspaper; cut out pattern 1" inside drawn line. Use pattern to cut one shape from poster board and two shapes from batting. Cut a fabric piece 2" larger on all sides than pattern. Glue both pieces of batting to one side of poster board. Place poster board, batting side down, on wrong side of fabric. Glue edges of fabric to back of poster board.

Continued on pg. 57

rag doll high chair

You will need a wooden high chair; blue, red, ivory, brown, black, flesh, and white acrylic paints; compressed craft sponge; paintbrushes; toothbrush; primer; non-toxic sealer; and any additional supplies listed in Step 1.

1. Read Preparing to Paint, Painting Your Chair, Sponge Painting, Transferring Patterns, and Painting Details, page 54.

2. Prepare chair for painting. Paint chair back, tray, and seat ivory. Paint legs, chair back rim, and armrest supports blue; paint armrests, rungs, and footrest red.

3. Cut a ³/₄" square and a 1¹/₄" square from craft sponge. Use the small square and blue paint to paint squares around edge of tray. Use the large square and red paint to paint squares on seat. Paint white dots on legs and chair back rim.

4. Transfer patterns, page 62, to chair back. Paint designs according to patterns. Use black paint to add "stitches" to hearts.

5. To spatter-paint chair, thin brown paint using water until it is an ink-like consistency. Dip toothbrush into thinned

Continued on pg. 57

liberty and justice for all

You will need a wooden spindle-back chair; red, navy blue, slate blue, and white acrylic paints; dark brown oil-based stain; glazing medium; assorted size star stencils; natural sponge; toothbrush; paintbrushes; fine-grade sandpaper; primer; sealer; and any additional supplies listed in Step 1.

1. Read Preparing to Paint, Painting Your Chair, Sponge Painting, Painting Details, Stenciling, and Antiquing, page 54.

2. Prepare chair for painting. Paint seat and chair back navy blue; paint legs red and leg rungs white. Paint chair back spindles red, white, and navy blue.

3. Use sponge and slate blue to lightly sponge paint seat and seat back.

4. Stencil navy blue, then slate blue and white stars on seat and seat back.

5. Transfer pattern, page 63, to seat back. Paint design white; outline using red.

6. Paint legs and leg rungs with checks, dots, and stripes. Sponge paint some white areas on legs using red and navy blue paints. To paint

Continued on pg. 57

heartland rocker

You will need a rocking chair with slatted seat; red, white, and blue acrylic paints; dark brown stain; paintbrushes; primer; sealer; and any additional supplies listed in Step 1.

1. Read Preparing to Paint, Painting Your Chair, Stenciling, and Antiquing, page 54.

2. Prepare chair for painting. Paint slats of seat red and white. Paint remainder of chair blue.

3. Use heart pattern, page 64, to stencil white hearts on chair.

4. Antique chair. Apply sealer to chair.

bright expectations

You will need a wooden chair with removable seat; bright blue, green, red, yellow, black, white, and dark pink acrylic paints; fabric for seat; batting; staple gun; liner paintbrush; paintbrushes; primer; sealer; and any additional supplies listed in Step 1.

1. Read Preparing to Paint, Painting Your Chair, Transferring Patterns, Painting Details, and Covering a Seat, page 54.

2. Prepare chair for painting. Referring to photo for color placement, paint chair.

3. Transfer pattern, page 64, to chair back. Paint design according to pattern.

4. Paint "S" strokes on chair back spindles using liner brush and yellow paint. Add dots, stripes, wavy lines, and comma strokes on remainder of chair using yellow, white, black, green, and red paints.

5. Apply sealer to chair.

6. Cover seat.

Designed by Diana Cates

happy hearts

You will need a ladder-back chair with rush seat; white, yellow, red, and green acrylic paints; ultra-thin craft steel; two 10" lengths of 20-gauge craft wire; paper crimping tool; craft knife; foam core board; paintbrushes; hot glue gun; black, permanent medium-point marker; two thumbtacks; primer; sealer; and any additional supplies listed in Step 1.

1. Read Preparing to Paint, Painting Your Chair, and Transferring Patterns, page 54.

2. Prepare chair for painting. Referring to photo for color placement, paint chair red, green, and yellow.

3. Paint white circles on chair back spindles and legs; paint yellow borders around circles.

4. Paint a yellow checkerboard on top rung of chair back. Use marker to write "Live each day with a happy ♥"; use white paint to add detail to heart. Paint a plaid design on second and bottom rung of chair back using red, white, and green paints.

5. Transfer heart pattern, page 64, to third rung of chair back; paint heart red and yellow. Outline heart using

Continued on pg. 60

feminine frills

You will need a wooden chair with removable back and seat; ivory, pink, dark pink, and light green acrylic paints; fabric to cover seat and seat back; satin fabric for chair skirt; iridescent tulle for chair skirt; $^3/_8$"w and $^5/_8$"w satin ribbon; silk roses; toothbrush; hot glue gun; paintbrushes; primer; sealer; and any additional supplies listed in Step 1.

1. Read Preparing to Paint, Painting Your Chair, Transferring Patterns, Painting Details, and Covering a Seat, page 54.

2. Prepare chair for painting. Paint chair ivory; paint selected details light green.

3. Transfer pattern, page 65, to chair back. Paint design according to pattern; use light green paint to add "tendrils" to design.

4. To spatter-paint chair, thin dark pink paint using water until it is an ink-like consistency. Dip toothbrush into thinned paint. Hold toothbrush next to chair surface; run thumb over toothbrush bristles to spatter-paint chair.

5. Apply sealer to chair.

6. Cover seat and chair back without using batting.

Continued on pg. 57

sweetheart seat

You will need a wicker chair; yellow, pink, blue, light green, and purple acrylic paints; whitewash spray; paintbrushes; primer; sealer; and any additional supplies listed in Step 1.

1. Read Preparing to Paint and Painting Your Chair, page 54.

2. Prepare chair for painting. Brush random splotches of paints onto various areas of chair until chair is covered with paints.

3. Spray chair with whitewash.

4. Apply sealer to chair.

Designed by Sandra Ritchie

home tweet home

You will need a wooden chair with removable seat; blue, gold, dark gold, red, black, white, brown, light green, and dark green acrylic paints; fabric for seat; batting; staple gun; black permanent pen; woodtone spray; natural sponge pieces; paintbrushes; primer; sealer; and any additional supplies listed in Step 1.

1. Please read Preparing to Paint, Painting Your Chair, Transferring Patterns, Painting Details, and Covering a Seat, page 54.

2. Prepare chair for painting. Paint chair blue.

3. Transfer pattern, page 66, to chair back support. Paint design according to pattern. Outline and add details using pen.

4. Paint vines and leaves on chair using light green and dark green paints.

5. Apply one light coat of woodtone spray to chair.

6. Apply sealer to chair.

7. Cover seat.

Designed by Diana Cates

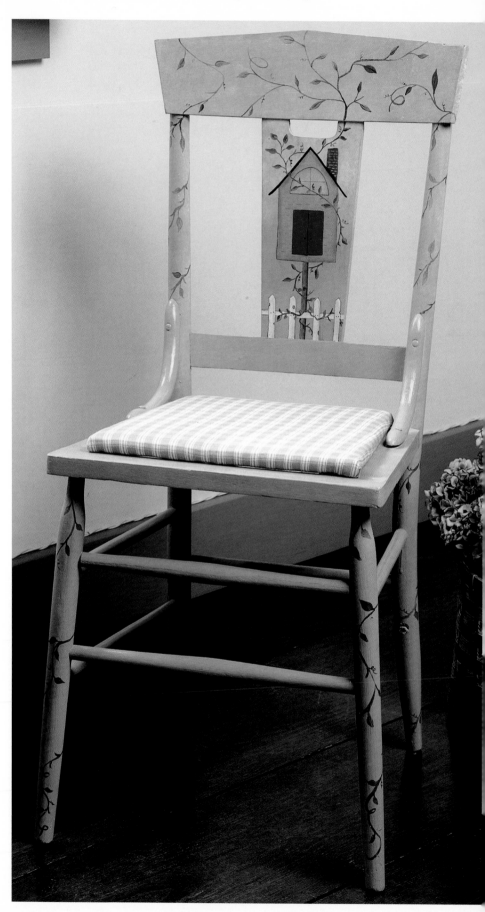

14

pretty in plaid

You will need a wooden spindle-back chair with removable seat; white, bright green, green, purple, dark purple, antique gold, bright blue, slate blue, and black acrylic paints; purple plaid fabric for seat; batting; staple gun; paintbrushes; natural sponge pieces; primer; sealer; and any additional supplies listed in Step 1.

1. Read Preparing to Paint, Painting Your Chair, Transferring Patterns, Painting Details, Sponge Painting, and Covering a Seat, page 54.

2. Prepare chair for painting. Paint chair white.

3. Thin purple paint using water. Paint diagonal stripes of various widths on chair back to imitate plaid pattern in seat fabric. Repeat with white paint.

4. Transfer outline of pattern, page 67, to chair back. Paint center of design white. Shade edges of design using slate blue, then bright blue; outline design using slate blue.

5. To paint flowers, transfer remainder of pattern, page 67, to center of painted outline. Shade all purple areas on design using purple; brush paint toward center of petals, using pattern as a guide.

Continued on pg. 58

winter wonderland

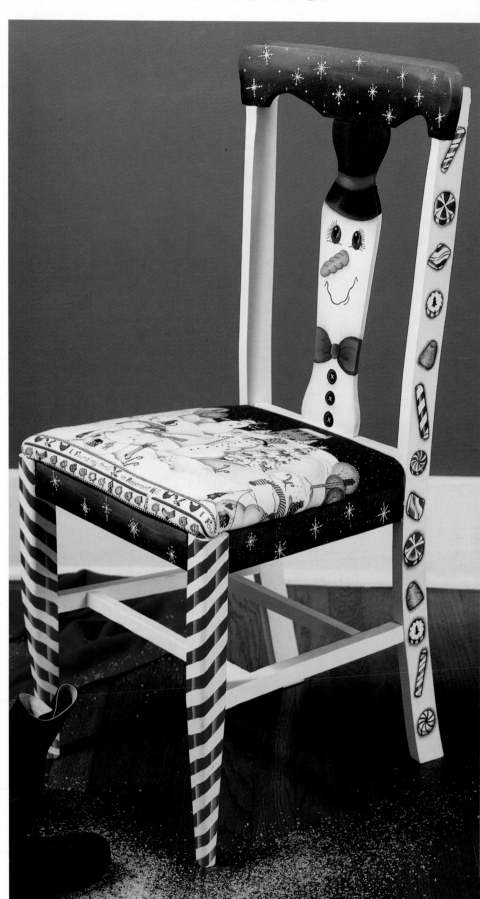

You will need a wooden chair; white, black, orange, dark blue, red, and green acrylic paints; fabric for seat; batting; staple gun; glazing medium; paintbrushes; natural sponge pieces; primer; sealer; and any additional supplies listed in Step 1.

1. Read Preparing to Paint, Painting Your Chair, Transferring Patterns, Sponge Painting, Painting Details, and Covering a Seat, page 54.

2. Prepare chair for painting. Paint chair white.

3. Transfer patterns, pages 68 and 69, to back and sides of chair. Paint candies according to pattern; use white paint to sponge paint down center of gumdrops. Outline candies using black paint. Shade around candies using dark blue paint; highlight inside of candies using white paint.

4. Paint snowman according to pattern. Use black paint to shade under hat and nose and around bow and buttons; shade around knot in bow. Use white paint to highlight hat, hatband, nose, bow, eye pupils, and buttons. Add details using white and black paints.

Continued on pg. 58

lovely ladybug

You will need a bentwood chair, black and green acrylic paints, red fabric to cover seat, batting, staple gun, paintbrushes, primer, sealer, and any additional supplies listed in Step 1.

1. Read Preparing to Paint, Painting Your Chair, and Covering a Seat, page 54.

2. Prepare chair for painting. Paint chair green and black. Apply sealer to chair.

3. Cover seat. Paint seat details using black paint.

Designed by Sandra Ritchie

fun fish

You will need a wooden chair; light blue, purple, orange, yellow, green, pink, light aqua, and black acrylic paints; three sided (small, medium, and large teeth) combing tool; paintbrushes; glazing medium; primer; non-toxic sealer; and any additional supplies listed in Step 1.

1. Read Preparing to Paint, Painting Your Chair, and Transferring Patterns, page 54.

2. Prepare chair for painting. Paint chair light aqua.

3. Mix glazing medium and light blue paint according to manufacturer's instructions. Apply glazing medium to chair back. Use combing tool to make "wave" pattern in glaze. Repeat for remaining chair parts.

4. Transfer patterns, page 70, to chair back, seat supports, and leg rungs. Paint designs according to patterns.

5. Apply sealer to chair.

Designed by Cherece Cooper

by the sea

You will need a wooden spindle-backed captain's chair; white, red, black, green, brown, tan, blue, light purple, and yellow acrylic paints; fabric for seat; 1" dia. white rope cording; cushion form to fit chair seat; mop brush; paintbrushes; natural sponge pieces; black, fine-point permanent pen; hot glue gun; primer; sealer; oak stain (optional); and any additional supplies listed in Step 1.

1. Read Preparing to Paint, Painting Your Chair, Transferring Patterns, and Sponge Painting, page 54.

2. Follow manufacturer's instructions to stain chair seat, if necessary. Prepare remaining chair for painting. Paint chair white; paint selected areas on chair back and spindles red.

3. Transfer star and word patterns, page 71, to chair back. Paint design black and red.

4. To paint design on chair back, lightly mark off a 17" x 3" oval on chair back. Using side to side strokes, paint bottom half of oval blue. Add white paint to blue paint to lighten; paint upper half of oval. Brush light purple paint around edges of upper half of oval. While paint is wet, stroke mop brush over design to soften.

Continued on pg. 58

"i love to sew!"

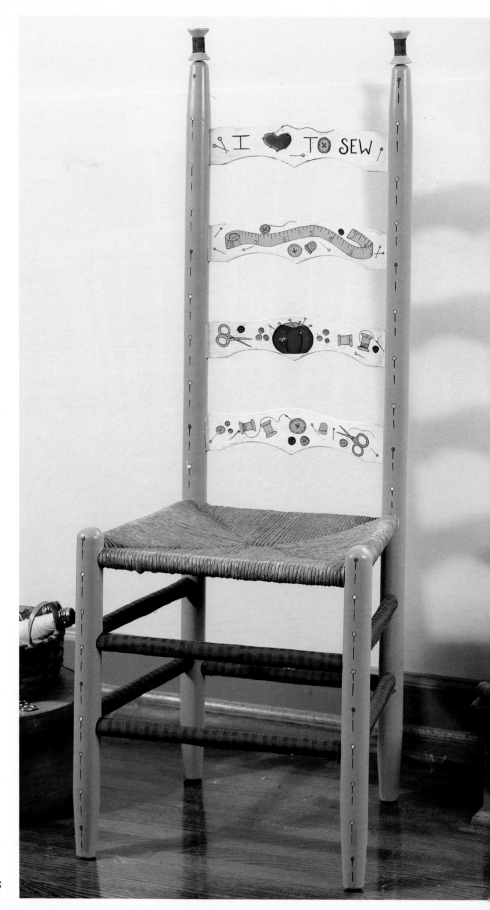

You will need a wooden ladder-backed chair; blue, white, red, black, green, and yellow acrylic paints; walnut stain; fabric to cover chair rungs and spools; two wooden spools; black, fine-point permanent pen; decoupage glue; cement glue; paintbrushes; primer; sealer; and any additional supplies listed in Step 1.

1. Read Preparing to Paint, Painting Your Chair, Transferring Patterns, Painting Details, and Antiquing, page 54.

2. Prepare chair for painting. Paint chair back rungs white; paint legs and chair back spindles blue. Paint spools yellow.

3. Transfer patterns, pages 72 and 73, to chair back rungs. Paint designs according to patterns. Paint "pins" on chair back spindles and legs using red, white, green, yellow, and black paints.

4. Antique chair back rungs and spools.

5. Apply sealer to chair.

6. Decoupage fabric around chair leg rungs and spools. Use cement glue to attach spools to chair back spindles.

Designed by Diana Cates

sportsman's dream

You will need a wooden chair with removable seat; medium ivory and brown acrylic paints; fabric for seat; staple gun; silk leaves; decoupage glue; natural sponge pieces; paintbrushes; primer; sealer; and any additional supplies listed in Step 1.

1. Read Preparing to Paint, Painting Your Chair, Sponge Painting, Antiquing, and Covering a Seat, page 54.

2. Prepare chair back and seat rim for painting. Paint chair back and seat rim medium ivory.

3. Sponge brown paint randomly over ivory areas. Use water to thin brown paint; use thinned paint to antique chair back and seat rim.

4. Decoupage leaves to chair. Use brown paint to highlight leaf veins.

5. Apply sealer to chair.

6. Cover seat without using batting.

bold black & white

You will need a wooden ladder-back chair with woven seat; white, black, and yellow acrylic paints; 2" length of ⁵/₈" dia. plastic tubing; paintbrushes; primer; sealer; and any additional supplies listed in Step 1.

1. Read Preparing to Paint, Painting Your Chair, and Painting Details, page 54.

2. Prepare chair for painting. Paint front legs, bottom leg rungs, and top and bottom chair back rungs black. Paint remaining chair white.

3. For circles on top and bottom chair back rungs, dip one end of plastic tubing in white paint; touch to surface of chair. Add black stripes to front chair leg rung and middle chair back rungs. Add black and white dots to legs and chair back spindles.

4. Paint seat yellow.

5. Apply sealer to chair.

Designed by Dani Martin

safari favorite

You will need a wooden arm chair; black, beige, ivory, medium brown, dark brown, and dark golden brown acrylic paints; walnut antiquing gel; paintbrushes; primer; sealer; and any additional supplies listed in Step 1.

1. Read Preparing to Paint, Painting Your Chair, and Antiquing, page 54.

2. Prepare chair for painting. Paint chair seat medium brown. Paint armrests and headrest beige. Paint chair back ivory. Paint legs, legs rungs, arm supports, and chair back spindles dark brown, ivory, black, and beige.

3. Paint large irregular shaped circles on seat using dark brown paint. Use black paint to paint irregular "V" shaped stripes on chair back. Paint small irregular shaped circles on armrests and headrest using dark golden brown paint; outline circles using black paint.

4. Antique chair. Apply sealer to chair.

Designed by Sandra Ritchie

elegant harmony

You will need a wooden harp-back chair with removable seat; taupe, dark brown, medium ivory, ivory, light brown, and metallic gold acrylic paints; fabric for seat; batting; staple gun; glazing medium; crackle medium; liquid gold leaf; mop brush; paintbrushes; natural sponge pieces; soft rag; rubbing alcohol; feather; toothbrush; primer; sealer; and any additional supplies listed in Step 1.

1. Read Preparing to Paint, Painting Your Chair, Sponge Painting, Stenciling, and Covering a Seat, page 54.

2. Prepare chair for painting. Paint harp dark brown; paint remaining chair taupe.

3. Mix equal parts medium ivory paint with glazing medium. Sponge mixture over taupe sections; blend using mop brush.

4. Following manufacturer's instructions, apply crackle medium over taupe sections. Mix equal parts metallic gold with glazing medium. Use rag to apply mixture over crackle medium.

5. Mix equal parts glazing medium with light brown, taupe, and medium ivory

Continued on pg. 58

splendid detail

You will need a wooden chair with removable seat; black, bright green, green, gold, and silver acrylic paints; glazing medium; $1/4"$ and $3/4"$ masking tape; paintbrushes; 1" sponge brush; small sponge roller; fabric for seat; batting; staple gun; heavy cardstock; primer; sealer; and any additional supplies listed in Step 1.

1. Read Preparing to Paint, Painting Your Chair, Painting Details, and Covering a Seat, page 54.

2. Prepare chair for painting. Paint chair back bright green; use sponge roller to paint remaining chair black. Add gold and silver details to chair legs, seat support, and chair back rails.

3. Tape off geometric design on chair back using masking tape. Cut a jagged edge on one side of cardstock.

4. Mix equal parts glazing medium and green paint. Use sponge brush to apply glaze mixture to one area of taped off design. Using a wavy stroke, drag jagged edge of cardstock through glaze mixture. Wipe glaze from cardstock. Allow each area to dry before painting the next section. Remove tape when all areas are dry.

Continued on pg. 59

faux sophisticated

You will need a wooden chair with removable seat; gold and brown acrylic paints; fabric for seat; batting; staple gun; oak, fruitwood, and walnut polyurethane stains; paintbrushes; primer; sealer; and any additional supplies listed in Step 1.

1. Read Preparing to Paint, Painting Your Chair, and Covering a Seat, page 54.

2. Prepare chair for painting. Paint chair back and seat support gold. Paint remaining chair brown.

3. Using paintbrush, randomly dab walnut stain on gold areas to be faux tortoise shell. While stain is wet, randomly dab on oak, then fruitwood stains. Add more walnut stain if needed. Check areas periodically as they dry, softening any drips by dabbing with paintbrush.

4. Once tortoise shell areas are dry, apply a light coat of walnut stain to tortoise shell and gold areas.

5. Apply sealer to chair.

6. Cover seat.

Designed by Ann Stocks

ornate oak

You will need a wooden chair with removable seat; antique gold and black acrylic paints; fabric for seat; staple gun; paintbrushes; dark oak stain; black upholstery gimp; bright brass upholstery tacks; hot glue gun; toothbrush; sealer; and any additional supplies listed in Step 1.

1. Read Preparing to Paint, Antiquing, Painting Details, Stenciling, and Making a Padded Seat, page 54.

2. Prepare chair for antiquing. Use stain to antique chair.

3. Use paintbrush and gold paint to stencil design, pages 74 and 75, on chair back. Add dots and comma strokes using black paint. Paint feet and rim of seat gold.

4. To spatter-paint chair, thin black paint using water until it is an ink-like consistency. Dip toothbrush into thinned paint. Hold toothbrush next to chair surface; run thumb over toothbrush bristles to spatter-paint chair.

5. Apply sealer to chair.

6. Make padded seat. Glue gimp around seat. Attach tacks to gimp.

Designed by Cherece Cooper

27

king's treasure

You will need a wooden arm chair with removable seat; dark gold, dark green, dark blue, medium purple, and dark purple acrylic paints; iridescent tinting medium; glazing medium; fabric for seat and chair back; batting; staple gun; wooden finials; gold cording; 1/4" dia. wooden dowel; drill with 1/4" bit; paintbrushes; heavy cardboard; hot glue gun; wood glue; primer; sealer; and any additional supplies listed in Step 1.

1. Read Preparing to Paint, Painting Your Chair, and Covering a Seat, page 54.

2. Prepare chair and finials for painting. Use drill and 1/4" bit to drill a hole at top of chair back spindles and in bottom of finials. Use wood glue to secure 1 1/2" lengths of dowel into holes at top of chair back spindles. Glue finials to dowels.

3. Paint chair back spindles, back legs, side leg braces, and front and back seat supports gold. Paint front legs and armrests green and dark purple. Paint armrest supports medium purple and blue. Paint chair back blue, medium purple, and green. Paint center leg rung medium purple. Paint finials green, gold, medium purple, blue, and dark purple. Paint side seat supports medium purple and blue.

Continued on pg. 59

fancy pansy

Continued on pg. 59

You will need a bentwood chair; dark green, bright green, light ivory, purple, dark purple, yellow, dark yellow, dark tan, and black acrylic paints; 1½"w paintbrush; paintbrushes; primer; sealer; and any additional supplies listed in Step 1.

1. Read Preparing to Paint, Painting Your Chair, Transferring Patterns, and Painting Details, page 54.

2. Prepare chair for painting. Paint seat light ivory; paint remaining chair bright green and dark green.

3. Transfer pattern, page 76, to seat.

4. Referring to pattern, paint purple, yellow, black, and dark tan areas on design. Paint remainder of seat bright green.

5. To paint purple area of design, refer to pattern and use 1½"w paintbrush and dark purple to shade all edges of area. Shade darkest areas several times, brushing paint down toward center of design. Without cleaning brush, use light ivory paint to highlight edge of top petal.

gone fishing

You will need a wooden ladder-back chair with removable seat; dark green, green, red, light tan, terra-cotta, gold, white, and black acrylic paints; fabric for seat; batting; staple gun; small fish net; braided raffia; 2³/₄" x 7" wooden plaque; 20-gauge craft wire; two 1¹/₄" dia. wooden ball beads; two 1" long wooden plugs to fit inside bead openings; paintbrushes; toothbrush; wood glue; cement glue; hot glue gun; primer; sealer; and any additional supplies listed in Step 1.

1. Read Preparing to Paint, Painting Your Chair, Transferring Patterns, Stenciling, Painting Details, and Covering a Seat, page 54.

2. Prepare chair, ball beads, and plugs for painting. Use wood glue to glue plugs into bead openings.

3. Paint chair dark green and beads red and white. Use cement glue to attach beads to top of chair spindles.

4. To stencil fish, page 77, paint fish light tan. Stencil design according to pattern using green, then terra-cotta, light tan, and gold paints. Add details using black paint; add dots using light tan, then black paints. Shade around each fish and next to chair back rungs using black paint.

Continued on pg. 59

woodland retreat

You will need a wooden ladder-back chair; tan, black, dark green, light green, brown, ivory, and reddish brown acrylic paints; paintbrushes; primer; sealer; and any additional supplies listed in Step 1.

1. Read Preparing to Paint, Painting Your Chair, Transferring Patterns, and Stenciling, page 54.

2. Prepare chair for painting. Paint seat and chair back rungs tan. Paint legs and chair back spindles light green; paint top of spindles reddish brown and tan. Paint leg rungs and seat supports reddish brown.

3. Transfer sawtooth pattern, page 78, to chair back rungs, legs, and seat. Paint designs reddish brown; paint a tan line around top of design on legs.

4. Stencil fish, tree, and bear according to patterns, page 78. Use brown paint to paint tree trunk and to outline and add details to fish.

5. Apply sealer to chair.

Designed by Linda Tiano

refreshing watermelon

You will need a wooden chair with removable seat; light green, medium green, dark green, white, black, pink, and dark pink acrylic paints; natural sponge pieces; white fabric to cover seat; batting; staple gun; paintbrushes; primer; sealer; and any additional supplies listed in Step 1.

1. Read Preparing to Paint, Painting Your Chair, Painting Details, Sponge Painting, and Covering a Seat, page 54.

2. Prepare chair for painting. Paint chair light green.

3. Sponge medium green vertical stripes on back of chair and around rim of chair seat support. Sponge medium green paint randomly on remaining chair.

4. Sponge dark green paint over center of vertical stripes.

5. Paint black and white stripes on chair rungs.

6. Apply sealer to chair.

7. Cover seat, but do not attach to chair. Sponge pink paint over entire surface of

Continued on pg. 59

rosy repose

You will need a wooden chair with removable seat; light green, pink, dark pink, white, dark green, and light tan acrylic paints; fabric for seat; batting; staple gun; paintbrushes; primer; sealer; and any additional supplies listed in Step 1.

1. Read Preparing to Paint, Painting Your Chair, Painting Details, and Covering a Seat, page 54.

2. Prepare chair for painting. Referring to photo for color placement, paint chair light green, dark pink, and light tan. Paint dark green dots on seat support.

3. Use dark pink paint to paint comma strokes on chair back and top front of legs. Highlight top of comma strokes using white paint.

4. Refer to photo and lightly mark placement of roses on chair back. For each rose, paint a dark pink $3/4$" long x $1/2$" wide oval. Thin pink paint using water. Use thinned paint to paint a second oval over dark pink oval; add a white dot to upper center of oval. Use light green paint to add two comma strokes to bottom of rose for leaves.

Continued on pg. 59

preschooler's choice

You will need a child's wooden folding chair; white, red, green, blue, yellow, black, silver, terra cotta, and dark flesh acrylic paints; paintbrushes; primer; non-toxic sealer; and any additional supplies listed in Step 1.

1. Read Preparing to Paint, Painting Your Chair, and Transferring Patterns, page 54.

2. Prepare chair for painting. Paint seat slats blue, green, and red; paint remaining chair white.

3. Transfer patterns, page 79, to chair back, seat, and sides. Paint letters and numbers red, green, and blue; paint remaining designs according to patterns.

4. Apply sealer to chair.

Designed by Dani Martin

noah's ark high chair

You will need a wooden high chair; white, black, yellow, orange, dark green, light green, dark brown, light brown, dark blue, light blue, and red acrylic paints; metallic gold paint pen; paintbrushes; primer; non-toxic sealer; and any additional supplies listed in Step 1.

1. Read Preparing to Paint, Painting Your Chair, and Transferring Patterns, page 54.

2. Prepare chair for painting. Paint tray using light green, light blue, and dark blue paints. Paint remaining chair dark blue. Transfer patterns, pages 80 and 81, to tray, footrest, and chair back.

3. Paint designs according to patterns. Use paint pen to outline designs and to add details.

4. Paint yellow and red diamonds and dots on chair back spindles. Paint black and white checks on edge of footrest and across top of chair back; use paint pen to add stripes to black checks. Use paint pen and red paint to add details to legs.

5. Apply sealer to chair.

baby's rainbow rocker

You will need a wooden spindle-backed rocking chair; blue, pink, purple, yellow, white, and green acrylic paints; natural sponge pieces; paintbrushes; primer; sealer; and any additional supplies listed in Step 1.

1. Read Preparing to Paint, Painting Your Chair, and Sponge Painting, page 54.

2. Prepare chair for painting. Paint a blue square on chair seat; paint chair back blue. Referring to photo for color placement, paint remaining chair.

3. Sponge yellow, pink, purple, and green paints on chair back to form rainbow.

4. Sponge paint white "clouds" over chair back, seat, and rockers. Sponge pink and yellow paints around blue square on chair seat.

5. Apply sealer to chair.

bee-blossom special

You will need a wooden folding chair; green, purple, blue, dark yellow, white, and black acrylic paints; paintbrushes; black, permanent medium-point marker; primer; sealer; and any additional supplies listed in Step 1.

1. Read Preparing to Paint, Painting Your Chair, Transferring Patterns, and Painting Details, page 54.

2. Prepare chair for painting. Paint chair white, green, and dark yellow.

3. Paint wavy green lines on chair back; paint green leaves and grass lines. Paint purple, blue, and yellow flowers at top of wavy lines.

4. Transfer pattern, page 81, to chair back. Paint design according to pattern. Use marker to add detail lines to design.

5. Apply sealer to chair.

dainty delft

You will need a wooden chair; bright blue and white acrylic paints; purchased blue and white cushion; paintbrushes; primer; sealer; and any additional supplies listed in Step 1.

1. Read Preparing to Paint, Painting Your Chair, and Transferring Patterns, page 54.

2. Prepare chair for painting. Paint chair white.

3. Transfer patterns, page 82, to chair. Paint design bright blue. Add small amount of white paint to blue paint to lighten; paint over outlines of design to soften edges.

4. Apply sealer to chair.

5. Tie cushion on chair.

Designed by Cyndi Hansen

38

lacy touch

You will need a wooden folding chair, white acrylic paint, blue spray paint, paper doilies and paper lace trim for stencils, stencil adhesive, paintbrush, primer, sealer, and any additional supplies listed in Step 1.

1. Read Preparing to Paint and Painting Your Chair, page 54.

2. Prepare chair for painting. Paint chair white.

3. Apply stencil adhesive to back of paper lace and doilies; press in place on chair.

4. Spray chair with paint, being careful not to spray under stencils. Allow to dry; remove stencils.

5. Apply sealer to chair.

Designed by Linda Tiano

"you are special!"

You will need a wooden arm chair with removable seat; hot pink, turquoise, orange, yellow, green, dark green, and black acrylic paints; fabric for seat; batting; staple gun; natural sponge; hot pink acrylic jewel stone; wooden carvings to fit back of chair; wood glue; jewel glue; paintbrushes; primer; sealer; and any additional supplies listed in Step 1.

1. Read Preparing to Paint, Painting Your Chair, Transferring Patterns, Painting Details, Sponge Painting, and Covering a Seat, page 54.

2. Prepare chair and carvings for painting. Use wood glue to attach carvings to chair back. Referring to photo for color placement, paint chair.

3. Sponge paint armrests and part of legs using hot pink and yellow paints. Add details such as hearts, squiggles, scallops, dots, lines, and comma strokes. Shade desired areas using dark green paint.

4. Transfer pattern, page 83, to front seat support. Paint design using black paint.

5. Use jewel glue to attach jewel to chair back. Apply sealer to chair.

6. Cover seat.

Designed by Dani Martin

coffee klatch

You will need a wooden chair; yellow, blue, turquoise, orange, pink, light green, green, dark purple, brown, and black acrylic paints; natural sponge pieces; paintbrushes; primer; sealer; and any additional supplies listed in Step 1.

1. Read Preparing to Paint, Painting Your Chair, Transferring Patterns, Painting Details, Sponge Painting, and Stenciling, page 54.

2. Prepare chair for painting. Paint chair yellow.

3. Paint squares on chair back supports using various colors of paint; paint dots in center of squares. Shade right-hand corner of squares at bottom of chair back using various colors of paint. Paint stripes and dots on chair legs.

4. Transfer coffee cups and coffee pot patterns, pages 84 - 86, to back of chair and chair seat support. Paint designs according to patterns.

5. Transfer word patterns, pages 84 - 86, to seat. Paint designs according to patterns.

6. Make stencil from coffee bean pattern, page 85. Sponge paint designs over chair seat and

Continued on pg. 59

You will need a wooden ladder-back chair with rush seat; white, blue, and yellow acrylic paints; paintbrushes; primer; sealer; paper towel; and any additional supplies listed in Step 1.

1. Read Preparing to Paint, Painting Your Chair, and Transferring Patterns, page 54.

2. Prepare chair for painting. Refer to photo for placement and transfer pattern, page 87, to chair back rungs, legs, and chair back spindles. Paint chair and design white, blue, and yellow. Paint blue "X's" on leg rungs.

3. Apply sealer to chair.

4. Paint seat blue. Dip paintbrush into white paint, then wipe off brush on paper towel until brush is almost dry. Paint seat with almost dry brush.

Designed by Linda Tiano

floral tradition

You will need a wooden chair with a removable seat; blue, purple, dark pink, white, yellow, brown, dark green, and light green acrylic paints; fabric for seat; batting; staple gun; paintbrushes; primer; sealer; and any additional supplies listed in Step 1.

1. Read Preparing to Paint, Painting Your Chair, Transferring Patterns, Painting Details, and Covering a Seat, page 54.

2. Prepare chair for painting. Paint chair white.

3. Transfer patterns, pages 88 and 89, to chair back and seat supports. Thin all paints to an ink-like consistency using water. Use thinned paint to paint designs according to patterns.

4. Use thinned paint to add wavy dark green lines on chair back spindles. Use thinned light green paint to add leaves to wavy lines.

5. Use undiluted paints to add details to leaves, basket, and flower buds. Add dots around flower centers and on all leaf stems.

6. Paint blue bands on chair back and lines on legs.

Continued on pg. 60

refreshing roses

You will need a wicker chair; light pink, dark pink, light green, dark green, light yellow, and ivory acrylic paints; paintbrushes; primer; sealer; and any additional supplies listed in Step 1.

1. Read Preparing to Paint and Painting Your Chair, page 54.

2. Prepare chair for painting. Paint chair light pink.

3. For roses, paint 4" dia. circles randomly over entire chair using light ivory paint. Paint over circles using light yellow paint. Paint light green leaves around roses.

4. Use dark pink paint to add detail lines to roses and to paint circles on chair. Use dark green paint to add detail lines on leaves.

5. Apply sealer to chair.

Designed by Anne Stocks

beribboned beauty

You will need a wooden chair with a removable seat; white, light blue, light red, and dark red acrylic paints; large floral design fabric for chair back and seat; batting; staple gun; glazing medium; natural sponge pieces; paintbrushes; decoupage glue; primer; sealer; and any additional supplies listed in Step 1.

1. Read Preparing to Paint, Painting Your Chair, Transferring Patterns, Painting Details, and Covering a Seat, page 54.

2. Prepare chair for painting. Paint chair back white. Referring to photo for color placement, paint remaining chair light blue and light red.

3. Transfer pattern, page 90, to chair back. Paint design light red. Using pattern as a guide, shade edges of design using dark red; add details and outline. Highlight remaining edges using white.

4. Shade edges of chair back using light blue paint.

5. Cut out floral design from fabric. Decoupage floral design to chair back.

Continued on pg. 60

rise and shine

You will need a wooden spindle-backed chair; yellow, red, white, and black acrylic paints; $^3/_4$" tall alphabet stencil; natural sponge piece; paintbrushes; primer; sealer; and any additional supplies listed in Step 1.

1. Read Preparing to Paint, Painting Your Chair, Transferring Patterns, Painting Details, and Stenciling, page 54.

2. Prepare chair for painting. Paint chair seat, center spindles, and lower part of chair back white; paint remaining chair, referring to photo for color placement.

3. Paint yellow dots on red areas and red dots on white areas. Paint red checkerboard on chair seat rim and lower part of chair back; paint black dots on white squares. Paint red lines on white center spindles.

4. Paint a 12$^1/_4$" long x 6$^1/_2$" tall yellow semi-circle on chair seat. Transfer "rays" patterns, page 91, around semi-circle; paint rays according to patterns.

5. Use alphabet stencil, sponge piece, and red paint to paint "Rise And Shine" and "Good Morning!" on chair back and seat.

Continued on pg. 60

wild, wild southwest

You will need a wooden mission-style chair with removable seat; red, white, yellow, orange, green, turquoise, and black acrylic paints; fabric for seat; batting; staple gun; paintbrushes; primer; sealer; and any additional supplies listed in Step 1.

1. Read Preparing to Paint, Painting Your Chair, Transferring Patterns, Painting Details, and Covering a Seat, page 54.

2. Prepare chair for painting. Paint chair back spindles yellow, turquoise, green, and orange. Paint leg fronts green and yellow. Paint remaining chair parts red.

3. Transfer patterns, pages 91 and 92, to chair back. Paint cactus and dogs green and black. Paint snakes according to photo. Use white, red, orange, and turquoise paints to add dots to snakes. Use yellow, orange, green, and turquoise paints to paint triangles on chair back and front seat support. Use black paint to add zig-zag line between triangles.

4. Apply sealer to chair.

5. Cover seat.

Designed by Cyndi Hansen

"thyme" for flowers

You will need a wooden chair with broken caned seat; light yellow, light purple, and grey-blue acrylic paints; paintbrushes; purple and green, permanent medium-point markers; clay flowerpot to fit in hole of seat; primer; sealer; and any additional supplies listed in Step 1.

1. Read Preparing to Paint, Painting Your Chair, and Transferring Patterns, page 54.

2. Prepare chair for painting. Paint chair light yellow, grey-blue, and light purple, referring to photo for color placement. Paint a 1³/₄" x 8⁵/₈" yellow rectangle with purple border on top chair back rung.

3. Transfer patterns, page 93, to seat back rungs. Use markers to draw over words and vines.

4. Apply sealer to chair.

5. Thin yellow paint with water. Paint flowerpot. Place flowerpot through seat of chair.

You will need a wooden ladder-back chair with removable seat; light yellow, dark yellow, green, purple, dark purple, orange, blue, and brown acrylic paints; fabric for seat and chair skirt; batting; staple gun; black, permanent fine-point marker; 1"w fusible web tape; paintbrushes; natural sponge pieces; primer; sealer; and any additional supplies listed in Step 1.

1. Read Preparing to Paint, Painting Your Chair, Transferring Patterns, Painting Details, Sponge Painting, and Covering a Seat, page 54.

2. Prepare chair for painting. Paint chair light yellow.

3. Transfer pattern, page 94, to top rung of chair back. For top wings on butterfly, brush blue paint from edge of wing toward center of wing, allowing some of the yellow background to show. Repeat for bottom wings using purple paint. Paint remaining design according to pattern. Outline design using pen. Shade around butterfly using dark yellow paint.

4. Apply one light coat of dark yellow paint to front of chair back spindles and where back rungs meet spindles. Lightly sponge paint green, dark purple, and

Continued on pg. 60

a profusion of posies

You will need a wooden chair with removable seat; grey-blue, purple, green, peach, and ivory acrylic paints; fabric for seat and to decoupage; upholstery foam; batting; staple gun; decoupage glue; paintbrushes; primer; sealer, and any additional supplies listed in Step 1.

1. Read Preparing to Paint, Painting Your Chair, and Covering a Seat, page 54.

2. Prepare chair for painting. Paint chair grey-blue.

3. Cut out motifs from fabric. Apply decoupage glue to back of motifs; smooth motifs onto chair. Apply decoupage glue over motifs.

4. Paint chair back purple and green with white details. Paint spindles purple, green, white, and peach. Paint purple and white details on seat supports and rung at base of chair.

5. Apply sealer to chair.

6. Cover seat.

garden party chair

You will need a wooden folding chair with removable seat; ivory, yellow, peach, deep red, dark green, light green, and metallic gold acrylic paints; fabric for seat; staple gun; gold and ivory upholstery gimp; hot glue gun; paintbrushes; primer; sealer; and any additional supplies listed in Step 1.

1. Read Preparing to Paint, Painting Your Chair, Transferring Patterns, Painting Details, and Making a Padded Seat, page 54.

2. Prepare chair for painting. Paint chair peach.

3. Use deep red paint to paint stripes on chair back top, outer spindles, and legs, dots on seat front, chair back, and chair back spindles, and wavy line on bottom rung of chair back. Paint over deep red details using gold paint, allowing red to show through slightly.

4. Transfer pattern, page 95, to chair back. Paint design according to pattern.

5. Apply sealer to chair.

6. Make padded seat. Use glue to attach ivory gimp around seat, covering edge of fabric. Repeat with gold gimp on top of ivory gimp.

Designed by Cherece Cooper

jungle fever

You will need a wooden chair with removable seat; purple, green, black, gold, tan, blue, and burgundy acrylic paints; fabric for seat; batting; staple gun; paintbrushes; primer; sealer, and any additional supplies listed in Step 1.

1. Read Preparing to Paint, Painting Your Chair, Transferring Patterns, and Covering a Seat, page 54.

2. Prepare chair for painting. Select spindle areas to be painted with animal print. Referring to photo for color placement, paint all remaining parts of chair with colors shown.

3. Transfer animal print patterns, page 96, to selected spindles; paint patterns tan and black. (If you desire, refer to patterns for design and freehand prints on spindles.) Paint black triangles on chair back. Paint blue and gold details on top of finials, and gold details on front legs and selected spindles.

4. Apply sealer to chair.

5. Cover seat.

Designed by Sandra Ritchie

You will need a child's wooden chair; dark blue, light blue, red, white, yellow, and dark green acrylic paints; black, fine-point permanent pen; paintbrushes; primer; non-toxic sealer; and any additional supplies listed in Step 1.

1. Read Preparing to Paint, Painting Your Chair, Transferring Patterns, and Painting Details, page 54.

2. Prepare chair for painting. Paint chair back rungs light blue. Use green, light blue, dark blue, red, and yellow paints to paint spindles. Paint chair leg rungs dark blue. Use white paint to add dots and stripes to spindles.

3. Transfer patterns, page 96, to chair back. Paint designs according to patterns. Paint a red and white striped border around house design. Use pen to outline designs and to add details.

4. Apply sealer to chair.

Choosing Your Chair

We used a variety of chairs for these projects. Some were new, unfinished pieces while others were older, flea market finds. Our instructions give you specific guidelines for painting the chair in the photo, however, if you can't find the exact chair pictured you can still paint the project. Just use the instructions as a general guideline to create your own unique chair.

Preparing to Paint

For safety's sake, carefully follow all manufacturers' instructions and warnings when using any cleaning, stripping, painting, or finishing product. For children's chairs, use non-toxic paints, primers, and sealers that are recommended for that purpose.

You may need household cleaner, oil soap, sponges, soft cloths, old paintbrush, toothbrush, paint/varnish stripper, wood putty, putty knife, wire brush, assorted grit or gauge sandpaper or steel wool, tack cloth, and items for repairing chair (hammer, screwdriver, drill, nails, screws, clamps, wood glue).

Preparation is the key. Before you paint, your goal is to have the chair in working condition, clean, and ready to accept paint.

1. Clean chair. Remove seat, if needed. Remove dirt, dust, and surface grime by cleaning it with a non-abrasive cleaner such as oil soap.
2. Prepare surface. The type of finish currently on your chair determines preparations.

Unfinished wood — Use fine-grit sandpaper to lightly sand entire surface.

Stained or stained and sealed surface — Use fine-grit sandpaper to lightly sand entire surface.

Painted surfaces in good condition — Use fine-grit sandpaper to lightly sand entire surface.

Painted surfaces in poor condition — Knock off any peeling or chipping paint with a wire brush. Smooth rough areas with medium-grit sandpaper, then go over entire chair lightly with fine-grit paper.

Painted surface with multiple paint layers — If your chair has many paint layers or the surface is lumpy or shows heavy brush strokes, your best option may be to strip the chair back to bare wood using a paint stripper. After stripping chair, make sure you lightly sand the entire surface.

3. Make repairs and remove hardware.
4. Wipe down chair using a tack cloth to remove dust.

Painting Your Chair

You may need masking tape, kraft paper, primer, paint (suggested in individual instructions or of your choice), and paintbrushes.

1. Mask off any area you don't wish to paint. Use masking tape and kraft paper as needed.
2. Apply a primer to your prepared surface before painting. Your paint will go on more smoothly and it will adhere better to your surface.
3. In most cases, you will need to paint the entire chair a single background color before you add decorative details. Apply paint using a paintbrush designed for the type of paint you are using, or you may use spray paint. Both types of paint may require more than one coat for even coverage.

Once the background color is dry, follow individual project instructions to paint details.

Transferring Patterns

You will need tracing paper, transfer paper, and a dull pencil.

Trace pattern onto tracing paper. Position tracing paper on surface; slide transfer paper between tracing paper and surface. Use a dull pencil to trace over all lines of the pattern.

For over-sized patterns, match dotted lines to complete pattern.

Painting Details

Dots — Dip the handle end of a paintbrush into paint. Touch end of paintbrush to surface.

Dot flowers — Make a circle of dots; add a dot in center of flower.

Shading and Highlighting — Dip flat paintbrush into water; blot on paper towel. Dip corner of paintbrush into paint. Stroke on waxed paper a few times to blend paint into brush. Stroke paintbrush on area to be shaded or highlighted (Fig. 1).

Fig. 1

Comma Strokes — Dip liner paintbrush into paint. Touch tip of paintbrush to surface, allowing brush hairs to spread out. Pull paintbrush toward you, lifting brush gradually as you pull to create the tail of the stroke (Fig. 2). For left or right comma strokes, pull the paintbrush to the left or right when you are creating the tail of the stroke (Fig. 3).

Fig. 2

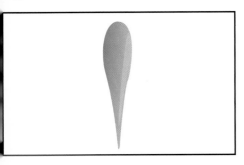

Fig. 3

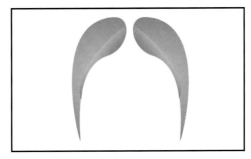

"S" Strokes — Dip flat paintbrush into paint. Touch flat tip of brush to surface. Pull brush to the left slightly and then down, applying pressure to flatten the brush hairs slightly. When stroke has reached the length you want, curve brush to the left again, raising brush back up gradually until only the flat tip of the brush is touching the surface (Fig. 4).

Fig. 4

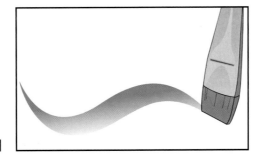

Sponge Painting

Lightly dip sponge into paint. Blot sponge on paper towel to remove excess paint. Press sponge onto surface; lift sponge straight up.

Stenciling

You will need sheet of stencil plastic; black, fine-point permanent pen; cutting mat or several layers of newspaper; craft knife; tape or stencil adhesive; paint(s); and stencil brush(es) or paintbrushes.

1. Cut a piece of stencil plastic 1" larger on all sides than pattern. Center plastic piece over pattern and use pen to trace outlines of pattern.
2. Place plastic piece on cutting mat and use craft knife to cut out stencil along pen lines.
3. Use stencil adhesive or tape to hold stencil in place while stenciling. Use a clean, dry brush for each color of paint. Dip brush in paint and remove excess paint on a paper towel. Brush should be almost dry to produce a good design.
4. If using stencil brush, begin at edge of cutout area and apply paint in a stamping motion. If using a regular paintbrush, begin at edge of cutout area and use a side-to-side sweeping motion to apply paint. Shade design by applying more paint around edge than in center. Carefully remove stencil.
5. To stencil designs in reverse, clean stencil with soap and water and dry thoroughly. Turn stencil over and stencil design.

Antiquing
You will need appropriate stain or paint, foam brushes, soft cloth, and paper towels.

Antiquing your chair gives the wood an aged appearance; it also softens the colors on your chair. The stain or paint can be applied to bare wood, over paint, or over a clear sealer. Test on an inconspicuous area of chair to assure desired results.

Working on one small area at a time, use a foam brush, paper towel, or soft cloth to apply stain or thinned paint to item; wipe immediately with a clean, soft cloth or paper towel to remove excess color. Let dry. Repeat as desired for darker color.

Covering a Seat
You will need fabric to cover seat, batting and/or upholstery foam, and staple gun.

1. Remove seat from chair. Draw around seat on wrong side of fabric. Cut out fabric 4" outside drawn line.
2. If using batting, cut batting same size as fabric. Layer batting, then fabric on seat. Fold fabric at corners diagonally over batting to fit seat corners. Alternating sides and pulling taut, staple edges of fabric to bottom of seat. Trim as necessary.
3. If using upholstery foam, cut foam same shape as seat. Wrap batting around foam to soften edges of foam piece. Layer foam, then fabric on seat. Wrap fabric around seat and staple edges to bottom of seat. Trim excess fabric.
4. Reattach seat to chair.

Making a Padded Seat
You will need fabric to cover seat; staple gun; and muslin to cover seat and fiberfill (optional).

1. Remove seat from chair.
2. If seat is already padded and covered, cut fabric 2" larger than area to be covered. Staple fabric around padded seat.
3. If seat is not padded and covered, cut muslin and fabric 5" larger than area to be covered. Staple muslin around three sides of seat area. Stuff fiberfill into seat area until padding is firm and slightly dome-shaped. Complete stapling around remaining side. Staple fabric over muslin. Trim muslin and fabric.
4. Reattach seat to chair.

delicate touches
page 4

two equal pieces; fold each piece in half and baste fold to right side of one fabric piece at tie marks. Use $1/2$" seam allowance to sew fabric pieces together, leaving an opening to turn and insert cushion form. Insert form; sew opening closed. Tie cushion to chair.

sunny flower garden
page 5

and legs. Paint designs according to patterns; use pen to outline leaves and add swirl to flower.

6. Use medium green paint to paint vines and leaves on center chair back spindles. Add pink dots to vines for roses; add white dots to center of roses. Paint remaining details on chair.

7. Apply sealer to chair.

Designed by Cyndi Hansen

quilt-patch rocker
page 6

6. For quilt-block appliqué, fuse web to wrong sides of all fabrics except muslin. Follow table to cut, then layer pieces in order listed. Fuse in place.

7. Fuse an $8^3/4$" square of web to wrong side of appliqué. Fringe edges of muslin to

edges of web. Fuse appliqué to cushion.

8. Glue welting to cushion, clipping seam allowance as necessary.

9. Sew buttons to cushion through all layers. Glue cushion to chair back.

Table for Quilt Block Rocker

Fabric Color	Size	# Needed
Muslin	$9^1/2$" square	1
Red plaid	6" square	1
Cream plaid	$1^1/2$" square	4
Blue check	$2^1/8$" square (then cut squares in half diagonally to make triangles)	2
Blue dot	$2^1/8$" square	1
Cream dot	$3/4$" square	4
Red stripe	1" x 6" strip	4
Blue dot	1" square	4

rag doll high chair
page 7

paint. Hold toothbrush next to chair surface; run thumb over toothbrush bristles to spatter-paint chair.

6. Apply sealer to chair.

Designed by Cyndi Hansen

liberty and justice for all
page 8

stars on legs, use white or navy blue paints and paint a small "x;" in center of "x," add a small dot of paint.

7. To spatter-paint chair, thin red paint using water until it is an ink-like consistency. Dip toothbrush into thinned paint. Hold toothbrush next to chair surface; run thumb over toothbrush bristles to spatter-paint chair. Repeat for navy blue and white paints.

8. To distress chair, use sandpaper and sand raised areas and around edges of chair.

9. Apply sealer to chair. Mix glazing medium with stain; antique chair. Apply a second coat of sealer to chair.

Designed by Dani Martin

feminine frills
page 12

7. To make chair skirt, measure from edge of chair seat to floor; add 2". Measure around chair seat; multiply measurement by two. Cut a strip of satin fabric and tulle the determined measurements. Using a 1" seam allowance, hem all sides of satin fabric strip. Fold one long edge of tulle 1" to wrong side (this will be the top of the chair skirt). Layer tulle on right side of satin fabric strip. To gather strip, sew long stitches along long edge (top) of strip, catching both tulle and satin fabric in stitching. Gently pull thread until fabric fits around chair seat. Glue strip around chair seat.

8. Holding both widths of ribbon, tie two bows. Glue bows to front of chair. Glue roses to center of bows.

---

pretty in plaid
page 15

Repeat shading using dark purple. Outline using dark purple.

6. Shade all blue areas on design using purple. Repeat shading using bright blue; brush paint toward center of petals, using pattern as a guide. Outline using bright blue.

7. Use black, white, and gold paints to add details to flowers.

8. Shade all leaves using green paint. Use green paint to add details.

9. Paint chair back spindles and front legs bright green, purple, and slate blue. Paint bottom chair back support bright green with purple stripes. Add purple wavy lines to front and back leg braces. Sponge purple paint on side leg braces. Add dark purple, bright green, and slate blue dots to seat, legs, and spindles.

10. Apply sealer to chair.

11. Cover seat.

Designed by Dani Martin

---

winter wonderland
page 16

5. Paint diagonal red stripes on legs; highlight center of each stripe using white paint.

6. Paint seat supports and top of chair back dark blue. Mix glazing medium and small amount of dark blue. To shade dark blue areas, begin at bottom of area and, using a side to side motion, paint upwards, gradually mixing small amounts of white paint into glaze to lighten color.

7. Add stars to front, sides, and top of chair using white paint.

8. Apply sealer to chair.

9. Cover seat.

Designed by Dani Martin

---

by the sea
page 19

5. Transfer boat and lighthouse patterns, page 71, to chair back. Paint designs according to patterns. Outline using pen.

6. Sponge paint brown, then tan paints at edges of oval. Sponge paint white "clouds" in upper half of oval.

7. Use white and black paints to add birds. Use brown paint to add tree trunk; sponge paint tree top using green paint. Use green paint to add grass.

8. Apply sealer to chair.

9. Place cushion form on wrong side of fabric; cut out two pieces of fabric 2" larger on all sides than cushion. Use 1/2" seam allowance to sew fabric pieces together, leaving an opening to turn and insert cushion form. Insert form; sew opening closed.

10. Beginning at center back of cushion, glue cording to cushion, tying four equally spaced knots in cording at front of cushion. Glue cushion to chair seat.

---

elegant harmony
page 24

paints. Beginning with darkest color, sponge each mixture diagonally across harp; blend using mop brush. While paint is still wet, use toothbrush to spatter harp with rubbing alcohol.

6. Mix equal parts ivory paint with glazing medium. Dip feather into paint and drag diagonally across harp, varying width and direction of lines to simulate marble veins.

7. Stencil pattern, page 73, on chair back using metallic gold. Use liquid gold leaf to paint details on chair.

8. Apply sealer to chair.

9. Cover seat.

Designed by Dani Martin

splendid detail
page 25

5. Use green paint to shade all inside and outside edges of design. Outline areas using gold paint. Paint gold and silver details on chair back.

6. Apply sealer to chair.

7. Cover seat.

Designed by Dani Martin

---

king's treasure
page 28

4. Mix three parts glaze with one part tinting medium. Paint chair with tinting medium.

5. Apply sealer to chair.

6. For padded back, cut cardboard oval to fit chair back. Cut three layers of batting same size as oval; hot glue batting to oval. Lay oval on wrong side of fabric; cut fabric 2" larger than oval. Hot glue edges of fabric to back of oval. Glue covered oval to chair back. Glue cording around oval.

7. Cover seat.

Designed by Dani Martin

---

fancy pansy
page 29

6. To paint yellow area of design, use 1¹/₂"w paintbrush and dark yellow to shade all edges of area. Shade darkest

areas several times, brushing paint up toward center of design.

7. Use black paint to outline and add details.

8. Paint "S" strokes and comma strokes on rim of seat using purple and yellow paints.

9. Paint yellow and purple dot flowers on chair back.

10. Apply sealer to chair.

Designed by Dani Martin

---

gone fishing
page 30

5. Paint plaque light tan. Transfer patterns, page 77, to chair back spindles and plaque. Paint designs according to patterns. Add details using black paint.

6. To spatter-paint chair, thin light tan paint using water until it is an ink-like consistency. Dip toothbrush into thinned paint. Hold toothbrush next to chair surface; run thumb over toothbrush bristles to spatter-paint chair.

7. Apply sealer to chair.

8. Cover seat. Hot glue braided raffia on front edge of seat.

9. Drape net over chair; hang plaque on chair.

Designed by Dani Martin

---

refreshing watermelon
page 32

seat cover. Lightly sponge white paint over pink paint. Sponge dark pink paint in center of seat cover. Use black paint to add comma stroke "seeds" to center of seat. Attach seat to chair.

Designed by Debra Smith

---

rosy repose
page 33

5. Apply sealer to chair.

6. Cover seat.

Designed by Diana Cates

---

coffee klatch
page 41

chair back using brown paint. Sponge black paint around edges of designs. Paint a black curved line down center of designs; outline designs using orange paint.

7. Apply sealer to chair.

Designed by Cherece Cooper

---

floral tradition
page 43

7. Apply sealer to chair.

8. Cover seat.

Designed by Linda Tiano

beribboned beauty
page 45

6. Mix equal parts glaze with white paint. Use sponge to lightly drag glaze over chair legs, seat supports, and chair back uprights.

7. Apply sealer to chair.

8. Cover seat.

Designed by Dani Martin

---

rise and shine
page 46

6. Apply sealer to chair.

Designed by Polly Browning

---

beautiful butterflies
page 49

orange paint down front of chair back spindles. Paint vines on spindles using green paint. To make flowers on spindles and chair back, use dark purple paint to make a circle of dots. Add an orange dot to center of flower.

5. Apply sealer to chair.

6. Cover seat, but do not attach to chair. For front skirt, measure front of seat; add 5½". Cut a piece of fabric 6¼"w by the determined measurement. For each side skirt, measure side of seat; add 3¼". Cut a piece of fabric 6¼" by the determined measurement. Press edges of each skirt piece ¼" to wrong side twice; stitch in place.

7. For front skirt, press two ½" pleats 3½" from each side of skirt *(Fig. 1)*. Following manufacturer's instructions, use ½" lengths of web tape to fuse top edges of each pleat together *(Fig. 2)*.

Fig. 1

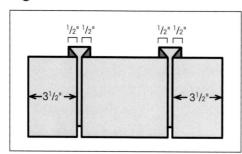

Fig. 2

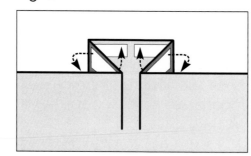

8. Press two ½" pleats at center of each side skirt. Use ½" lengths of web tape to fuse top edges of each pleat together.

9. Staple top edge of each skirt piece to bottom edge of seat. Replace seat.

---

happy hearts
page 11

6. Use craft knife and heart and star patterns, page 64, to cut hearts and stars from foam core and craft steel. Use crimping tool to corrugate steel heart and star. Paint foam heart and star yellow and red. Glue steel heart and star to foam heart and star.

7. Wrap each length of wire around marker to curl. Insert one end of each wire into a foam shape. Wrap remaining end of wire around thumbtack. Insert thumbtacks into top of chair spindles.

8. Apply sealer to chair.

Designed by Sandra Ritchie

sunny flower garden
(page 5)

flower for chair seat

flower for chair back and legs

leaves for
arm rests
and center
leg braces

check for center
leg brace

check for chair seat

check for arm rests

rag doll high chair
(page 7)

Enlarge pattern(s) to fit chair. Leisure Arts, Inc., grants permission to the owner of this book to photocopy the designs on this page for personal use only.

liberty and justice for all
(page 8)

Liberty and

Justice

for All ..

heartland rocker
(page 9)

happy hearts
(page 11)

bright expectations
(page 10)

feminine frills
(page 12)

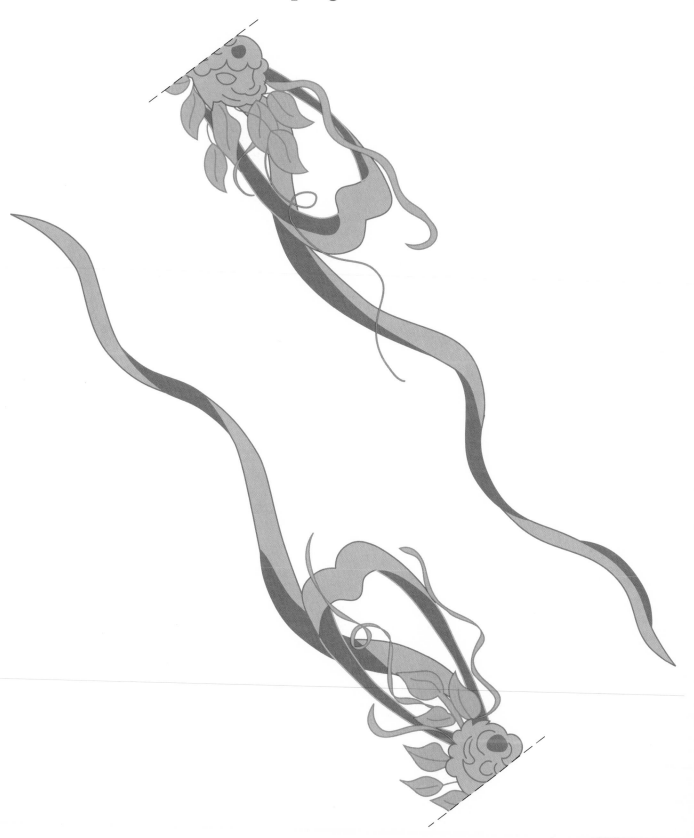

home tweet home
(page 14)

Enlarge pattern to fit chair. Leisure Arts, Inc., grants permission to the owner of this book to photocopy the designs on this page for personal use only.

pretty in plaid
(page 15)

Reduce pattern to fit chair.
Leisure Arts, Inc., grants permission to the
owner of this book to photocopy the
designs on this page for personal use only.

winter wonderland
(page 16)

Enlarge pattern to fit chair. Leisure Arts, Inc., grants permission to the owner of this book to photocopy the designs on this page for personal use only.

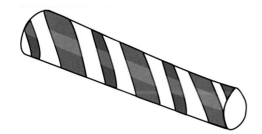

fun fish
(page 18)

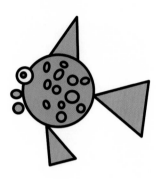

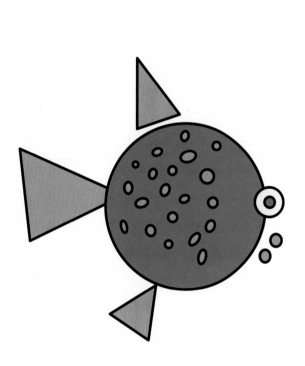

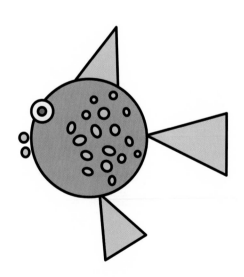

by the sea
(page 19)

BY THE SEA

BY THE BEAUTIFUL SEA

"i love to sew!"
(page 20)

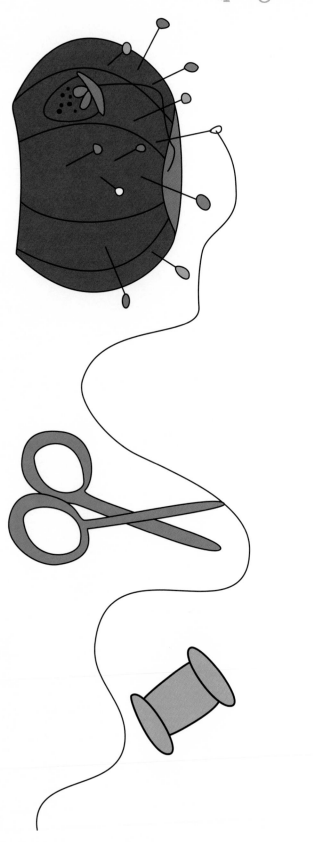

I

TO

SEW

elegant harmony
(page 24)

ornate oak
(page 27)

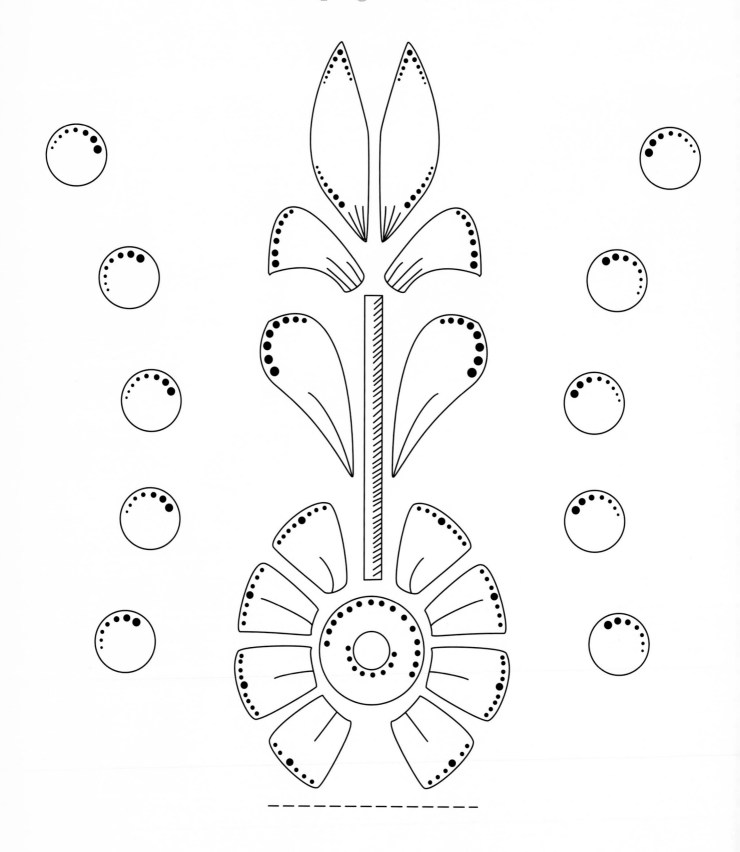

ornate oak
(continued)

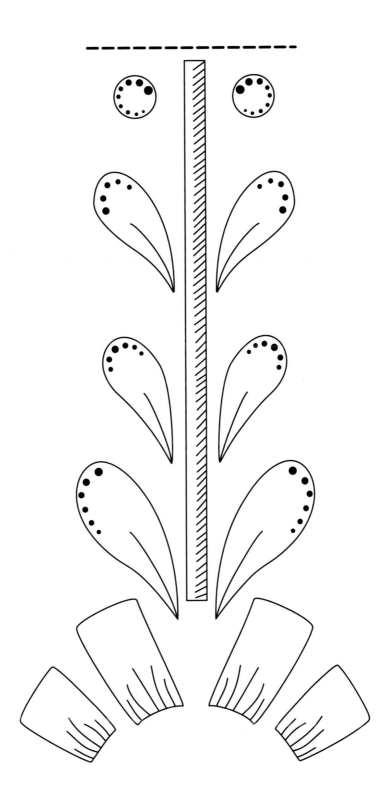

fancy pansy
(page 29)

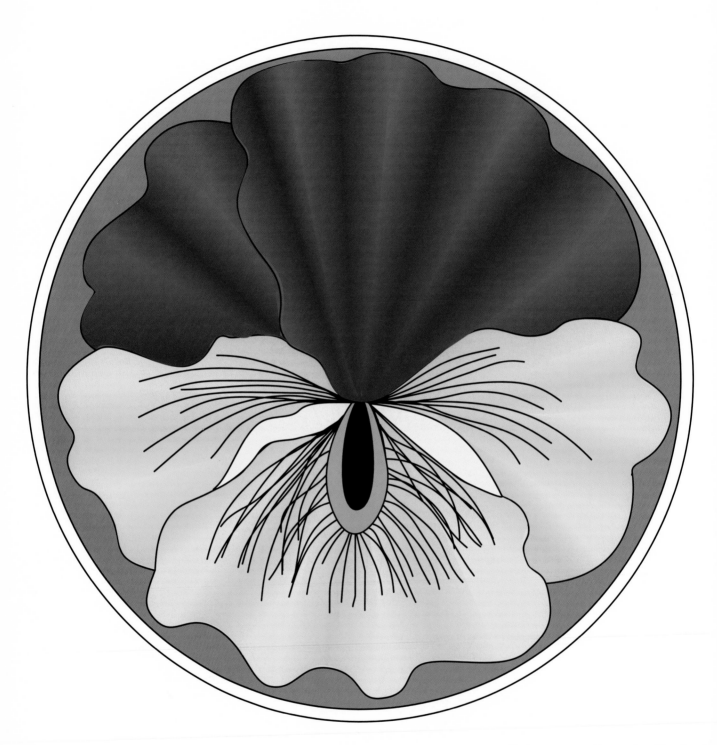

Enlarge pattern to fit chair. Leisure Arts, Inc., grants permission to the owner of this book to photocopy the designs on this page for personal use only.

gone fishing
(page 30)

Gone Fishing

woodland retreat
(page 31)

preschooler's choice
(page 34)

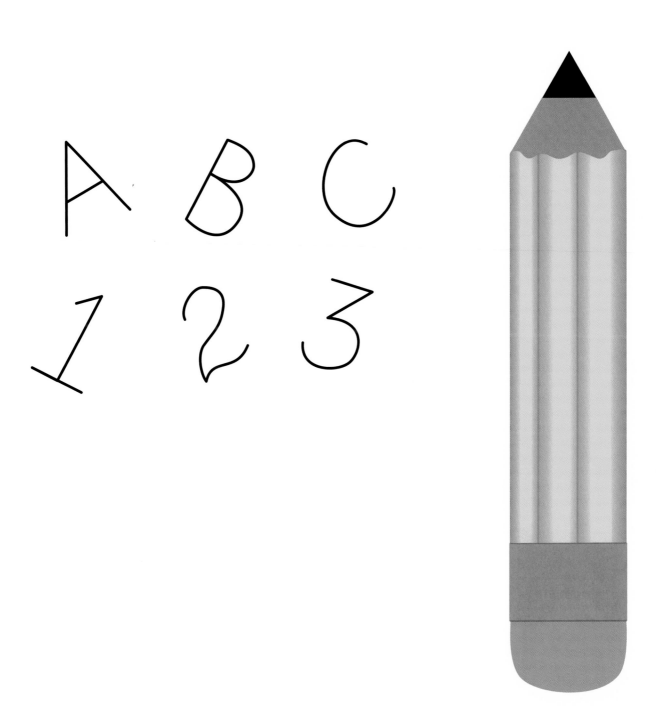

noah's ark high chair
(page 35)

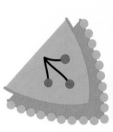

noah's ark high chair
(continued)

bee-blossom special
(page 37)

dainty delft
(page 38)

Enlarge pattern(s) to fit chair. Leisure Arts, Inc., grants permission to the owner of this book to photocopy the designs on this page for personal use only.

"you are special!"

(page 40)

Cappuccino

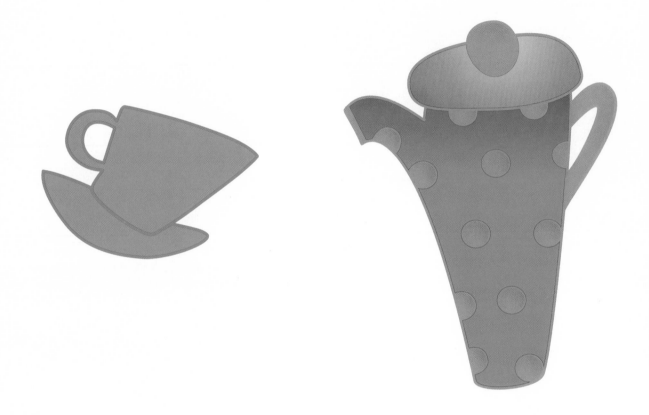

Espresso

floral tradition
(page 43)

Enlarge pattern to fit chair. Leisure Arts, Inc., grants permission to the owner of this book to photocopy the designs on this page for personal use only.

floral tradition
(continued)

Reduce pattern to fit chair. Leisure Arts, Inc., grants permission to the owner of this book to photocopy the designs on this page for personal use only.

beribboned beauty
(page 45)

Enlarge pattern to fit chair. Leisure Arts, Inc., grants permission to the owner of this book to photocopy the designs on this page for personal use only.

rise and shine
(page 46)

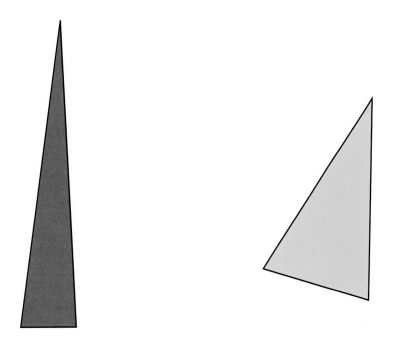

wild, wild southwest
(page 47)

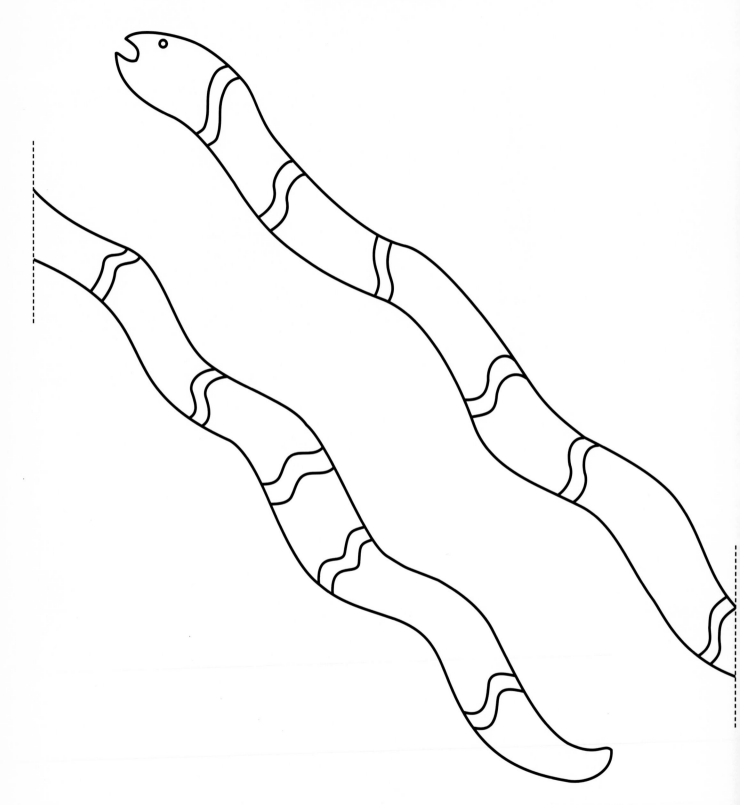

"thyme" for flowers
(page 48)

Take Thyme

To Smell

The Flowers